Country Puddings and Pies

traditional
recipes for fruit, milk
and bread puddings and
sweet and savoury pies
by

Bobby Freeman

Grandmother's Rice Pudding

Pwdin Reis Mam-gu

All rice puddings were once as delicate and appealing as this, but Victorian times brought about the survival of the much inferior 'servants'' or 'Nursery' rice pudding. Eliza Acton's recipe for 'Rice Pudding Meringue' in *Modern Cookery for Private Families* (1845), is similar to this:

50g / 2 oz rice
50g / 2 oz Demerara sugar
600ml / 1 pint rich Jersey milk or single cream
25g / 1 oz butter
2 whole eggs & 2 egg whites
300ml / ½ pint water
4 tablespoons caster sugar
nutmeg, pinch salt

Simmer the rice in the water until the grains are swollen. Add milk or cream, butter, sugar and salt and nutmeg, and the beaten yolks of 2 eggs.

Whisk the 4 egg whites until stiff, folding in the sugar. Pile the meringue on top of the pudding and bake in a moderate oven (350ºF, Gas 4, 180ºC) for half an hour, until the meringue is pale and biscuity.

Violet Pudding
Pwdin Fioled

Before chemical flavourings and colourings were
developed, flowers – especially violets, roses and
marigolds – were commonly used by both cottagers and
gentry. In the great houses and mansions 'syrops' were
made from violets and roses, and the petals preserved
by crystallising (painted with egg-white, sugared and
dried in the sun) until the manufacturers took over. This
violet-flavoured custard is a Radnorshire farmer's wife's
recipe:

6 handfuls fresh or crystallised violets
6 eggs
1 tablespoon runny honey
juice of a lemon

Boil the violets in a little water (enough to prevent them
sticking) until they are tender. Beat the eggs to a froth
with the honey and lemon juice. Bake in a greased dish in
a really low oven (250–300ºF, Gas ½–2, 130–150ºC) until
set – about 1 hour, but check after ¾ hour. Serve with
fresh violet petals sprinkled over the top,
and plenty of cream.

Owain Glendower's Lemon Pudding

Pwdin Lemwn Owain Glyndŵr

'so named (and Anglicized!) by Sir Robert Howell Vaughan,
Bart., the <u>real composer</u> Certain.'

From a MS cookery book of the late 18th century by
Elizabeth Baker, the invaluable secretary at Hengwrt, the
Vaughan mansion near Dolgellau, the town where the
heroic Welsh freedom fighter, crowned Prince of Wales,
held one of his two parliaments. This is a modern
adaptation:

3 lemons (juice & zest)
3 tablespoons chopped suet
14 tablespoons white breadcrumbs
6 tablespoons caster sugar
3 tablespoons white wine or cider
1 egg yolk
currants

Mix all the ingredients together, adding the eggs last, and
either fill small well-greased ovenproof dishes or one
large dish and bake, covered, in a *bain-marie* in a
moderate oven (350°F, Gas 4, 180°C) for ¾ hour, or longer
for the single dish.

Sauce: butter, white wine, sugar and lemon juice boiled
together for a few minutes.

Sir Watkin Williams Wynne's Pudding

Pwdin Watcyn Wynne

A famous old bread pudding from the Welsh border family whose name is much in evidence along the Cheshire/Shropshire border with Wales. The original used the once-popular beef marrow. Suet can be substituted.

125g / 4 oz suet
125g / 4 oz sugar
125g / 4 oz breadcrumbs
1 lemon
2 eggs, separated

Grate the rind of the lemon, strain the juice. Add the beaten egg yolks to all the other ingredients, then fold in the stiffly-beaten egg whites. Steam for 2 hours in a mould or buttered basin.

Serve with a sauce of 2 egg yolks, 1 tablespoon sugar, 1 tablespoon brandy, rum or whisky, 2 tablespoons warm water whisked over a low heat until stiff. Use immediately.

Prince of Wales' Cream

Cwstard Tywysog Cymru

A Victorian recipe, origin unknown, but typical of the many delicate little lemon desserts of the time. The custard will curdle if the milk is too hot for the eggs, and the same risk applies if the mixture is not really cool before the lemon juice is added.

850ml / 1½ pints milk
3 well-beaten eggs
12g / ½ oz gelatine
225g / ½ lb sugar
juice of 2 lemons

Dissolve the gelatine in the milk. Add the sugar and the thin peel of the lemon. Boil for 5 minutes. Cool, gently add the eggs. When almost cold, add the lemon juice and strain into one mould or individual glasses.

Snowdon Pudding
Pwdin Eryri

Eliza Acton gave the 'genuine' recipe in 1845, asserting that it was 'constantly served to travellers at the hotel at the foot of Snowdon' – the 'Pen-y-groes'.

225g / ½ lb suet
450g / 1 lb breadcrumbs
40g / 1½ oz rice flour
175g / 6 oz lemon marmalade
175g / 6 oz pale brown sugar
6 eggs
2 lemons
some fine stoned raisins

Butter a quart mould or basin thickly. Ornament it with the raisins pressed well into the butter. Mix the dry ingredients, then blend with the well-beaten eggs. Put in the basin and boil 1½ hours. Serve with a wine sauce as for the lemon puddings on p.5.

Quince Fool
Hwfen Cwins

This once plentiful fruit can still be obtained in some places in Britain. The fruit should be cut in quarters but not peeled, and steamed, covered, until they are soft, and then sieved and sweetened with caster sugar. As with all fruit fools, simply fold fresh double cream into the cold fruit purée. Suitable quantities would be:

450g / 1 lb quinces
175g / 6 oz caster sugar
175ml / ⅓ pint approx. double cream

A recipe similar to this appears in a notebook kept by a Mrs Owen of Penrhos in 1695.

Apple & Ginger Fool
Hwfen Afal a Sinsir

'I often think of apple and ginger fool, and plum pie and medlar trifle.'

One of Richard Llewellyn's memories recalled in *How Green Was My Valley* – a simple enough dessert lifted out of the ordinary by spicing with ginger. Powdered ginger can be used, but the syrup from stem ginger is better.

675g / 1½ lbs Bramley cooking apples
225g / 8 oz caster sugar*
300ml / ½ pint double cream
ginger to taste

*less if ginger syrup is used

Peel the apples and stew in a minimum amount of water, sweetening and spicing the hot pulp. When quite cold, fold in the cream. Serve with thin ginger biscuits.

Welsh Pudding
Pwdin Cymreig

At one time all baked puddings were encased in puff pastry – our baked custard tarts of today are a reminder. This old recipe found its way into Warne's *Model Cookery* an inexpensive Victorian cookery book. It is extremely extravagant, even allowing for the fact that eggs were smaller in the 18th century when the dish must have originated.

225g / 8 oz butter
8 small egg yolks
4 small egg whites
175g / 6 oz sugar
peel of a lemon
puff paste

Gently melt the butter, beat the yolks into it, then the sugar, then fold in the stiffly-beaten whites. Add grated lemon peel. Line an ovenproof dish with puff paste, pour in the mixture and 'nicely bake it' in a moderate oven (375ºF, Gas 5, 190ºC) for about 1 hour.

Monmouth Pudding

Pwdin Mynwy

Many old puddings bear the name of a town – the historic old county town of Monmouthshire (now in Gwent) seems to have been the only Welsh town with this distinction.

225g / 8 oz white breadcrumbs
300ml / ½ pint milk
2 tablespoons granulated sugar
2 tablespoons butter
2 egg whites
nutmeg
red jam or pie filling

Boil the milk, pour over crumbs, cover and leave for 10 minutes. Break up with a fork, work in the sugar, butter, nutmeg, and finally the stiffly-beaten egg whites. Put a layer of jam on the bottom of a greased glass soufflé dish, then a layer of crumb mixture. Repeat. Bake, covered, for about 30 minutes at 350°F, Gas 4, 180°C. Then liberally cover the top with brown or white sugar and caramalise under a hot grill. Serve slightly warm with plenty of cream.

Eve's Pudding
Pwdin Efa

The soufflé topping to this apple-based pudding means it must be eaten straight from the oven, for it collapses very quickly.

stewed apples, sweetened
50g / 2 oz plain flour
25g / 1 oz sugar
40g / 1½ oz butter
2 eggs
300–425ml / ½–¾ pint milk

Grease a deep, straight-sided ovenproof dish and cover the bottom with a generous layer of stewed, sweetened apple.

Melt the butter in a saucepan, stir in the flour and add the milk a little at a time to make a smooth sauce. Pour into a bowl and add the sugar and egg yolks. Finally, fold in the stiffly-beaten egg whites. Pour over the apples. Bake for ¾ hour in a fairly hot oven (425°F, Gas 7, 220°C).

Patagonia Carrot Pudding

Pwdin Moron Patagonia

Being unaware of their earlier use, most cooks greeted with derision the instruction to use carrots to eke out the sugar ration in the last war. When carrots are used in puddings and cakes it is for their sweetness, and the recipe is an old one from the time when sugar was scarce and dear. The older the carrots the more sweetness they contain.

1 cup grated carrot
1 cup grated potato
1 cup raisins
1 cup flour
1 cup sugar
½ cup melted butter
½ teaspoon bicarbonate of soda
2 teaspoons cinnamon
pinch salt

(These are American cups holding 8 fl. oz / 225ml)

Mix the bicarbonate of soda with the potato. Add the raisins to the flour, then add all the other ingredients and mix together thoroughly. Turn into a greased basin, cover the top with foil or greaseproof paper and boil for about 2 hours.

Gooseberry Pudding
Pwdin Gwsberen

A simple, old-fashioned pudding that's quickly made
when there's no time for anything more elaborate.

600ml / 1 pint stewed gooseberries
125g / 4 oz sugar
2 eggs
25g / 1 oz butter
125g / 4 oz brown breadcrumbs

Sweeten the gooseberries with the sugar, add the butter
and breadcrumbs and cool. Stir in the well beaten eggs.
Pour into a buttered baking dish and bake 30 minutes in
a moderate oven (375°F, Gas 4, 180°C). Strew sugar over
the top before serving.

Apple Brandy Pudding
Pwdin Afal Brandi

From Anne Hughes' diary (see p. 29)

450g / 1 lb cooking apples
225g / 8 oz dark brown molasses sugar
225g / 4 oz suet
125ml / 4 fl. oz brandy & 2 tablespoons
175g / 6 oz brown breadcrumbs
3 eggs
double cream

Soak the crumbs in the 125ml / 4 fl. oz of brandy. Core the apples but do not peel. Slice very thinly. Cover the bottom of a deep ovenproof dish with slices, then cover with sugar and a little suet, then a layer of soaked crumbs. Repeat. Beat the eggs with the 2 tablespoons of brandy until well frothed, then pour over the layered mixture. Bake for 30 minutes in a moderate oven (350°F, Gas 4, 180°C). Cool and chill before covering the top with spoonfuls of beaten double cream.

Trollies
Trolis

The first name is more or less slang for the proper Welsh
name (omit the 't' and the meaning becomes clear and
the Scandinavian connection disappears). In English they
would be called dumplings. They come from the old
Welsh rural tradition – made with oatmeal and boiled in
with the broth they were eaten as 'fillers' when potatoes
were scarce and dear.

175g / 6 oz self-raising flour
50g / 2 oz suet
50g / 2 oz currants
pinch salt, nutmeg
milk to mix

Combine all the ingredients and mix to a stiff dough with
the milk. Mould into balls or rounds and flatten to about
¾ inch thick. Coat each in flour, then drop one by one
into a saucepan of boiling water. They take about 20
minutes. Served hot with a spoonful of brown sugar and
a knob of butter on each, they were a pudding.

Blackberry Bread Pudding
Bara Mwyar

This is one of my favourites. So simple, yet so deliciously different, it has charmed and intrigued the most sophisticated gourmets – the perfect example of the great Escoffier's enjoinder to *faites simple*.

Quantities are immaterial. You need:

blackberries
sugar
stale bread

Set the blackberries to stew over a low heat and, when the juice is flowing nicely, add sugar to taste. Now throw in pieces of torn bread (a mixture of half white and brown is much the best) until the juice is all but absorbed – not too much bread or the result will be stodgy. Make sure the bread is well-broken up. Chill very thoroughly and serve with plenty of double cream.

This pudding can be made just as successfully with tinned or frozen blackberries.

Quarryman's Favourite
Ffefryn Chwarelwr

Many traditional dishes evolve from workpeople's need for portable food to eat at their workplace. Cornish pasties are one example. This was popular with the slate quarrymen of north Wales:

450g / 1 lb flour
225g / ½ lb lard
225g / ½ lb currants
125g / ¼ lb sugar
pinch salt
few dabs butter

Make pastry with the flour, lard and salt. Divide in two, roll out fairly thinly and cover a large oven plate with one half. Spread the currants evenly over the pastry, dot with butter and sprinkle with sugar. Cover with the rest of the pastry, seal the edges, cut air holes in the top. Brush with milk and egg and cook to golden brown (425ºF, Gas 7, 220ºC).

Rhubarb Shortcake

Teisen frau Riwbob

A Glamorganshire recipe

Prepare a few sticks of rhubarb and cook them with a
tablespoon of water and a little sugar – either in the oven
or slowly in a saucepan until just tender.

For the shortcake:

350g / 12 oz flour
125g / 4 oz butter
50g / 2 oz sugar
1 teaspoon baking powder
1 egg
milk to mix

Add baking powder to flour and rub in butter. Add sugar.
Mix with egg and milk to a stiff consistency. Divide in
two. Roll one half out to an oblong, ¾ inch thick and lay
on a greased baking sheet. Spread with rhubarb. Roll out
the other half and place on top. Bake in a hot oven
(425°F, Gas 7, 220°C) for 25 minutes. Cut in slices
when cool.

Cheese Pudding
Pwdin Caws Pobi

An interesting and unusual supper or lunch dish – the final development of Welsh rarebit perhaps? (*Caws pobi*, as it is in Welsh, was originally a slice of cheese laid on the untoasted side of a piece of bread and then toasted.)

4 thick slices crustless bread
225g / 8 oz Cheddar cheese
1 egg
600ml / 1 pint milk (or ½ milk, ½ cream)
butter
cayenne pepper
pinch nutmeg

Toast the bread on one side, butter the other side. Place two slices, toasted side down, on the bottom of a greased ovenproof dish. Grate the cheese and spread half over the toast, season. Repeat. Boil the milk, add seasonings and beaten egg. Pour over the pudding, leave to soak at least half an hour. Bake in a moderate oven (350°F, Gas 4, 180°C) until risen and pale gold on top.
Serve at once (2–4 people).

Patagonia Cream Tart
Teisen Hufen Patagonia

A rich dish designed to use the surplus of dairy produce which resulted when the Welsh settlers finally succeeded in damming the River Camwy.

225g / 8 oz flour
125g / 4 oz butter
3 eggs, separated
300ml / ½ pint double cream
1 tablespoon vanilla sugar

Rub the butter into the flour and bind with the egg yolks to a rich paste. Rest it for several hours before rolling out to line a fairly deep pie dish.

Beat the egg whites until stiff, fold into the cream with the sugar (use essence if vanilla sugar is not available), sprinkle nutmeg on the top and bake in a low oven (325ºF, Gas 3, 170ºC) for 35–40 minutes.

Dowset
A Gower dish

There were several versions of this open baked tart, often made in the bread oven after the bread had been removed. Some are like egg custard tarts; this one has a slight resemblance to Bakewell tart.

6 tablespoons plain flour
½ teaspoon baking powder
2 teaspoons sugar
1 egg
225g / 8 oz shortcrust pastry
jam

Line a pie dish with pastry. Spread jam over the bottom. Make a batter with the flour and sugar etc. and pour into the pastry case. Bake in a fairly hot oven (375ºF, Gas 5, 190ºC) for about 30 minutes or until golden.

Cranberry Tart
Tarten Llugaeron

Cranberries (tiny versions of their cultivated American cousins) grow wild in upland regions of Wales, underneath other plants on wet, boggy land. This recipe is from Radnorshire – I have not come across it in any other region so it is reasonable to suppose that only in that area were the berries accessible from habitations.

450g / 1 lb cranberries
225g / 8 oz raisins
25g / 1 oz sugar
275g / 10 oz rich shortcrust
½ teaspoon vanilla essence

Put the first three ingredients in layers in a basin and leave overnight. Next day, turn into a saucepan, bring slowly to the boil, simmer for 5 minutes. Add vanilla and leave to cool. Now make a plate tart with the pastry and fruit and bake in a hot oven (425°F, Gas 7, 220°C). Eat hot or cold, but always with cheese.

Marrow Pie

Tarten Bwmpen

Most Welsh recipe collections include one for marrow in a pie – spiced and often mixed with a little apple. Be careful not to add water as the marrow supplies a lot of moisture:

1 marrow
cupful sugar
cupful currants
sprinkle vinegar
pinch ginger
a few cloves
shortcrust pastry

Peel and slice the marrow, discarding seeds. Line a deep pie dish with shortcrust, fill with slices of marrow. Add sugar, currants, vinegar, spices, cover with a pastry lid. Bake in a moderate oven (325°F, Gas 3, 170°C) until the marrow is cooked – take care the pastry does not overcook. Alternately, cook the marrow first, drain, and bake the pie in a hotter oven.

Katt Pies

As there is no 'k' in the Welsh alphabet, this name is a
tremendous puzzle, although the pies were indeed
associated with Templeton Fair (12 November) in
Pembrokeshire. Explanations on lines of 'pussy pies' are
not allowed!

Mutton pies like these, spiced and sweetened with
sugar and dried fruits (originally made thus to disguise
the taste of tainted meat) were long favourites with the
British. A version of Katt pie is made, with other Welsh
dishes, at the White Hart, Cenarth, by the famous falls
near Cardigan.

450g / 1 lb flour
175g / 6 oz suet or lard
150ml / ¼ pint milk & water
good pinch salt
225g / ½ lb minced mutton or lamb
225g / ½ lb currants
225g / ½ lb brown sugar
salt & pepper

Make a hot water crust by melting the fat in boiling milk
and water – pour liquid into a well of flour and mix with a
wooden spoon until cool enough to handle, then shape
to pies 4 inches in diameter. Arrange filling in layers –
meat, fruit, sugar, seasoning as you go. Cover with a
round of pastry. Bake 30 minutes in a hot oven (425°F,
Gas 7, 220°C). Eat hot.

May Day Pie

Pastai Calan Mai

From Anne Hughes' diary

With her husband John, Anne Hughes worked a prosperous farm near Chepstow around the turn of the 18th century. In 1796 she kept an account of the year's day-to-day events of which she was very much the warm-hearted hub. The diary is full of recipes, mostly imprecise but capable of interpretation.

These little meat and fruit pies were made 'reddie for who shall cum amaying tomorrow, it being maye day'. They were fashioned like Cornish pasties, the mixture of cooked meat (probably mutton or lamb), apples and pear 'chopt very fine with a bit of union, sum lemmon tyme and a bit of rosemarie', seasoned with pepper and salt and a 'sprinkel' of dark brown sugar being laid on one half of a small circle of firm pastry. Then wet the edges and 'turn one side atop the other, and press with hands to make them stick'. Brush with beaten egg and bake for 30 minutes in a hot oven (425°F, Gas 7, 220°C).

Leek Pasty

Pastai Cennin

Although the leek is, with the daffodil, one of the emblems of Wales, the extraordinary fact is that there are very few dishes in the Welsh repertoire which actually feature it. This is one – simple and good:

225g / 8 oz shortcrust (225g)
2 or 3 medium leeks
4 rashers streaky bacon

Line a baking plate or shallow pie dish with half the shortcrust. Cover with the leeks, finely chopped and using a little of the innermost green. Lay the strips of bacon on top, season, moisten with an egg-cup of water, then cover with a pastry lid, making slits in the top. Bake in a fairly hot oven (400°F, Gas 6, 200°C) for 30–40 minutes. Serve hot. I like to add a little chopped fresh sage, and sometimes a beaten egg or two instead of the water to moisten the pasty.

OVEN TEMPERATURES			
Low	240°–310°F	115°–155°C	Gas ¼–2
Moderate	320°–370°F	160°–190°C	Gas 3–4
Fairly Hot	380°–400°F	195°–205°C	Gas 5
Hot	410°–440°F	210°–230°C	Gas 6–7
Very Hot	450°–480°F	235°–250°C	Gas 8–9

Also in the series:
A Book of Welsh Country Cakes and Buns
A Book of Welsh Bread
A Book of Welsh Bakestone Cookery
A Book of Welsh Fish
A Book of Welsh Soups and Savouries

Also by Bobby Freeman:
Lloyd George's Favourite Dishes (1974, 1976, 1978 – Ed.)
Gwent – A Guide to South East Wales (1980)
First Catch Your Peacock: The Classic Guide to Welsh Food
(1980)
Welsh Country House Cookery (1983)
*Welsh Country Cookery – Traditional Recipes from the
Country Kitchens of Wales* (1987)

First impression: 1984

ISBN: 978-1-78461-894-0

Published and printed in Wales on paper from well-maintained
forests by Y Lolfa Cyf., Talybont, Ceredigion SY24 5HE
e-mail ylolfa@ylolfa.com
website www.ylolfa.com
tel 01970 832 304
fax 832 782